GONE TOO SOON

GONE TOO SOON

LAURA EVANESKI

ITI Music Corporation

iti
Music Corporation

ITI Music Corporation Publishing

16057 Tampa Palms Blvd West

Tampa, FL 33647

ISBN: 978-0-9995684-4-6

Printed and bound in the United States

Cover: RoxC LLC/www.roxc.graphics/Roxanne Clapp

All Photos: Courtesy of the Evaneski Family

This book is dedicated to John Evaneski.

Thank you to my husband and writer Michael Dion for his encouragement and help in putting this book together. (You can find this book, along with his books and Jazz Label at www.itimusic.live)

Thank you to Bill Jakub for hearing me out and keeping me on the path.

Thank you to Phil Ribera for his emails about my Dad. He is also a great writer – please check out his books.

Thank you to My Daughter for always expecting the truth.

And finally, Thank you to My Sisters for Their Love.

INTRODUCTION

GONE TOO SOON

Late September 2018, I received a text message from my middle sister saying, "Call me, I have wildly interesting news."

Being the curious person that I am, I called her right-away.

She told me that a man called her looking for me about a letter I had written to him in 1994 and that he felt bad that he'd never responded to me.

My sister gave me his phone number and email address and within minutes I had typed out an email reply to him.

I told him that I knew I couldn't call him because I would be too emotional but I wanted him to know what an impact he had made on my family and how important he was to my father.

I had to go to an appointment that I had scheduled for the day and afterwards when I looked down at my phone after clearing my calendar, I saw that I had a missed call from him.

After all these years, was he really searching me out?

Was it a hoax?

Two days earlier I was having inner turmoil whether I should write this book. I had started and stopped it so many times, over the years, that ranged from concentrating on the murders or the direction I have chosen to go into that has also been shaped by the twenty-five plus years since the senseless crime, as well as the early years that helped shaped this man.

It's a very personal thing to write about the life, escapades and eventual murder of your own father. However, truth be told, I really didn't know my Father very well.

In the end, you'll have to tell me what you think?

Was it the right thing to do?

GONE TOO SOON

Chapter 1

"The Crime Scene"

Assess the scene. Save the savable. The Oakland Fire & Rescue had a horrifying situation on their hands. Years later, one of the paramedics on the scene wrote a book where he discussed what happened that night. That the man that he treated was still alive, but unlikely to make it, so they used their training and saved the savable.

I know the training and understand it but still, I am open about my anger.

What if?

Just in the past couple of weeks as I worked on this book during October-November 2018, there were three mass shootings.

When did this become commonplace?

More importantly, how are we going to stop it?

When this took place, I know my Dad had these thoughts running through his head:

"Are you freaking kidding me? Like this? No gunfight? No super cop that saves the day? No not even close."

From everything that we know he was the first to be taken out. People later said he wouldn't have wanted it any other way. (Though I would have!).

They went on to say, that he never would've wanted to die of old age or be sick.

I call bullshit on that. He was only 51 years old and just starting his third career: Navy Electrician, Police Officer and then Disc Jockey.

There was a radio station in the Bay area of which I can't remember the call letters that John would sometimes sit in as a guest DJ. He loved being on the air. It was part of his persona.

He even created a song out of "Mack the Knife" with all of the radio personalities names. He was a creative man and liked to sing and had a nice voice.

GONE TOO SOON

Chapter 2

"The Call 1992"

My telephone rang around 4 AM on February 19th. My Mother was on the other end of the line.

She said, "Laura, your father is dead."

In hindsight, I am grateful for the simplicity of the statement. There was no wonder or hope or wish or prayer. There was simply a finality. Your Father is dead. Shot, murdered, gone!

"We will never have the opportunity to fix the many shattered pieces of our relationship", I remembered thinking.

We three Sisters lives were "Shattered on Shattuck."

This is what I learned initially, Tuesday night at approximately 9:25 PM, two males entered the Bos'n Locker on Shattuck Avenue in Oakland, California. The bar was well known for locals playing darts & listening to R&B and Reggae, dancing and eating the House specialty, "Jerk Chicken". It was the kind of place that you took your kid for their first drink.

It was a Tuesday evening and it had rained day and night for ten days.

The ground was slick but not as slick as the blood-soaked floor of the Bos'n.

The two young men carrying Uzis were literally inside the small bar for a matter of minutes firing nearly 100 rounds. Eleven people were shot or wounded that night and three died.

Many asked in the days following the shooting why the retired cop was not caring a gun. In fact, he was. A little pearl-handled revolver.

He once said to me that he was just crazy enough to bite someone's nose off if they bothered him.

However, what he faced that night was unimaginable.

He waited so long to be able to start this new career. He had had business cards made, and his Astro van was covered with Jamaican beauties along with his DJ contact information that he initially called himself "Vito Z" but later renamed himself "Brother John".

These were the very early days of CNN. Twenty-four-hour cable news was something brand new and this was a big story for them.

The news coverage was vast as they did interviews with patrons that were overcome by grief. They showed them removing the body bag containing my father and I remember seeing the screen as his name appeared larger than life.

Then the video showing the outline of my father's body and thinking to myself, "How callous it was".

As I've gotten older, I have a love-hate relationship with the news. On one hand, I want to be informed but the panic and sometimes anger that it instills in me is often not worth it.

There is no sound description of the wailing pain when you have been given news like that. Though forty apartments on Palm Canyon Drive in Palm Springs California claimed to have heard me that early morning. The night before, I sat on the floor in front of the TV drawing with colored pencils, feeling bad for myself that I had made such a mess of my life, not knowing it was my Dad's final day.

This is the reason I never feel sorry or pity for myself. It was up to me to change my situation, no one else.

GONE TOO SOON

Chapter 3

"I need to go to the Funeral"

That morning, I remember calling my boss to let him know I would need to travel to the Bay Area and was told that I could not leave work as the owner's dog had passed away.

I had worked at a jewelry store within a high-end hotel on Frank Sinatra Drive in Rancho Mirage.

Among the rich and the famous and the wannabees, the bighorn sheep were free to roam into the hotel and when they would consume whole bushes of Bougainvillea, the talented landscape team would be right behind them to refresh the gardens as if they had never been touched.

Though it was a major chain, lots of celebrities stayed there and were constantly wandering throughout the property.

One day, Donald Trump and Marla Maples were there and I ran into her in the bathroom. When I walked out, he, Donald, was standing against the wall and in those days without any entourage.

Later, they came into the jewelry store to look around. They were all over the tabloids at this time and were likely hiding out in the desert.

Another time, I heard a booming voice behind me and turned to find OJ Simpson and Marcus Allen.

It was the type of place where selling $170,000.00 vintage platinum and sapphire Art Deco sets was not out of the norm. On Sundays, I would be expected to be there at work for 12 hours, even after the hotel had quieted down.

Downstairs, underneath the hotel main floors, the staff treated each other with the same proper greetings as they did upstairs with the guests.

I still say "my pleasure" to this very day.

During this time, and as a naïve young woman, I was the only one working between my husband and myself. Since I didn't want to lose my job, I opened the shop almost daily because the Frenchman who owned the store insisted that I do so.

When I arrived, Gabriel Barda had set up a shrine for his dog "Senior", with photographs, fresh cut flowers, and a candle. It was the epitome of selfishness.

Though he didn't care what had happened in my life, many staffers came by to make sure I was ok. They knew something was wrong, since I wore sunglasses all day, as my eyes were swollen.

GONE TOO SOON

Chapter 4

"Harold"

Harold Robbins is best known as the writer of the "Carpetbaggers" in 1961, but his first novel was "Never Love a Stranger" in1948. It was a novel about the American film industry from its beginning to the sound era. His books were often based on drama, sex, and glossy high society. Harold once told me how he got into writing. He had become an executive with Universal Pictures studios and would read the books that came in for consideration for a film adaptation.

When reviewing the financials for the films, he would think, "I can write crap better than this".

Harold first befriended me when I started working in the jewelry store. He told me he enjoyed coming to the hotel for lunch but had serious issues about the pricing of life's most basic supplies. He once told the hotel management that "paying twenty-five dollars for eleven cents worth of pasta was outrageous? I must be in the wrong business!"

Harold and I were both thrifty people, who liked to discuss "The Art of Frugality", even though I didn't drive that beautiful white Rolls-Royce that he did.

That day, within two hours of my arrival and a phone reservation in the dining room, Harold was made aware of my situation.

"Aren't you friendly with Laura in the jewelry store?" asked the waiter.

"Have you heard the news?", he continued.

Down the hallway of the hotel, Harold Robbins was seen pushing his wheelchair as fast as it would go and burst into the jewelry salon and said to Gabriel, "What the fuck is going on?"

Harold was a favored guest of the hotel and restaurant and carried a lot of weight, throughout the Palm Springs area.

Harold had married Jann just five days earlier on Valentine's Day and should have been celebrating but instead, he was fighting for my basic rights as a human being.

Turning his wheelchair around, he went directly to the hotel director office and insisted that I be allowed to leave and travel to attend my Father's funeral. He also demanded that I be put up at a proper San Francisco location. No one messed with Harold Robbins.

Now gone these many years, Harold died on October 14th, 1997, in Palm Springs California. Prior to his death, he spent a great deal of time on the French Riviera, particularly in Monte Carlo, until his passing from respiratory heart failure at the age of 81.

I must say that I loved him and miss his banter. He was gruff, sincere and generous.

I was married at the time, a sham that I entered into at a young age. I was 22, and he was 37 and from a once wealthy Jewish family.

When I met him, he was all smoke and mirrors. In all honesty, I likely got what I deserved. Running away to California from Cape Cod to escape a life of mistakes with a man I didn't know.

When I met him, I was working at a hotel on The Cape. The eighties were a time before bad behavior and an overactive libido got you into much trouble.

We partied and tried recreational drugs and danced the nights away. I was a bartender and cocktail waitress from the time I was 18 years of age.

I say I likely got what I deserved because by the time I met him I had given up on having a successful life or the hopes of having any more than I currently had.

On my way to meet Larry, in Las Vegas, I traveled from Cape Cod to the San Francisco Bay Area to see my Dad. He picked me up at the airport and I went to his house for a few days.

I was newly sober the first time, and at twenty-two-year-old dealing with her father.

Sober much less, Dad's concern was that I was going to run up his phone bill. He asked me why I was making this move and why wasn't this guy coming to my Dad's house to retrieve me?

In my mind, I figured moving to California with a man I dated 4 days and talked to on the phone three weeks was just another gamble. Unfortunately, I lost...

Once moving to LA, Larry went to work as the National Sales Manager for his friend's mini blind company. He called on the various Hollywood studios and helped outfit the set of "Dallas".

At the time, we lived in Playa del Rey. I did not know how to drive so I took a bus into Marina Del Rey daily to work at a tanning salon frequented by celebrities.

Larry's job lasted only four months until he decided the nine to five didn't agree with him and he quit, leaving his good friend since childhood, in the lurch.

But I continued to take the bus five days a week into the Marina to help pay the rent and be out of the studio apartment.

GONE TOO SOON

Chapter 5

"What to Wear?"

I can think of the shock on the faces of the department store staff as I looked for something to wear to the funeral.

Do I wear a hat?

"Can I assist you", asked the sales gal from behind the counter?

"Hmmm, well let's see. My Father has been murdered, shot to death actually by an automatic assault rifle.

What does one normally wear to that?

WTF?

"What was wrong with me?"

As if the shock factor I'm using against this innocent salesperson was going to ease my grief or my own shock and daze that I was walking around in.

I am ashamed of myself to say, that was not the only incident.

In the end, I bought nothing. I may have worked full time but I had no money of my own. I was kept on a very short leash, just like a dog.

I had spent 10 years being driven to and from work. I never had any money of my own.

I continued to work in very upscale stores, like Saks Fifth Avenue. And with a markdown or discount and only a few pieces of clothing, I was able to pull it off.

When we moved to the desert, Mr. Barda hired me right off the floor of Saks 5th Avenue in Palm Springs.

There too, we lived in a studio apartment and the only way I got any alone time was when I was not at work, sitting in a very small bathroom.

Of course, he told everyone he was tied into the Las Vegas "family" and worked for a billionaire and we lived on his property. He also told everyone that he traveled in his Lear jet with " Nicky". Even though Nicky did not exist and Larry did not leave his recliner.

My every move was tracked and I was not allowed to speak to my family.

There I said it.

Before my Dad was murdered, his last voicemail to me was "Fuck you, Laura!"

Don't get me wrong, my father loved me but he certainly was upset with my choice of spouses, and he didn't particularly like me at that time.

When my husband started trouble about an upcoming family event my Dad had had enough. So he left me that voicemail. So now you know. We weren't even talking, and five months of silence had passed.

Then Dad was gone.

GONE TOO SOON

Chapter 6

"Attending the funeral"

Larry tried to verbally massacre my emotional being to not attend my Father's funeral. I fought tooth and nail the entire way.

I remember thinking, sitting in the front row of the Chapel of the Chimes in Hayward. "I am here Dad. I made it."

We arrived only a few short hours before the funeral was to start.

There were two police officers standing watch, one on each side of his casket. One of them almost looked like Dad when he was young and I thought my eyes were playing tricks on me. In my state of shock, it looked to me like he was a younger John looking over himself.

There was a couple sitting right behind me, a biker and his wife. They both wore heavy worn leathers and sported tattoos. He had a freshly shaven bald head and was kind of stocky, sitting there with an Elvis compact disc in his hand.

Turning to him, I asked him, "How did you know my Dad?"

He replied, "I just traveled from Connecticut to attend the funeral of my murdered friend."

He then told me a story that I'd heard in different variations from people throughout my entire life.

My Dad would call people out of the blue and ask in his game show voice, "Do you know who this is?"

He would give the person a clue or two as to how they knew him, as it was a genuinely a pretty easy guess.

He loved to do that, surprise people. I think that's where I get it from.

The biker then went on to say, that they grew up together, in the streets of Norwalk.

Dad never forgot where he came from. He never forgot who he was. And he never judged others or the choices they made in their lives.

I asked the biker about the Elvis CD, what did it represent? He said, "Your Dad despised Elvis, and if I had brought him Roy Orbison, it would have made him too happy."

Inside, hundreds of people attended the funeral, along with many people listening from the steps outside.

There were city and state officials, retired and active officers of the Hayward Police Department. And there were criminals, who Dad had arrested.

Unsure, there was a large police presence as far as security went. No one knew at that moment if all of the people involved in the murder were accounted for.

There was also some biker gangs that showed who wanted to cause trouble and came inside to write terrible things on the book for the family.

In the end, they were not arrested because basically they did nothing illegal but they were removed from the property.

Because Dad spent much time in Ocho Rios, so many Jamaicans from the island as well as locals, came to the funeral. He had traveled there much over the years and brought supplies, blankets, and radios to share among his island family.

Some might ask, "Why would I write this book after twenty-five plus years since my Father's murder?"

Well, when a series of events trigger your life, you stand up and take notice and realize you need to write it down. No one can deny that Life is a full circle.

This true story is about a funny driven street cop that rose through the ranks.

Stories that appeared on CBS news with Walter Cronkite. Outrageous busts and the emotional toll that some of these events took on this controversial yet well-liked man.

GONE TOO SOON

Chapter 7

"Johnny was a good boy"

Johnny grew up in the blue-collar town of Norwalk Connecticut. As it stands today, Norwalk is an up-and-coming revitalized town with cute shops and eateries but back in the 1950s, it was the town of tough workers and a hard life.

Dad spent the first 10 years of his life in Washington Village. A Federal housing project where an alley separated the two cultures and races.

Dad once said that these shaped his biases early on, but the years in the Navy and in public service changed his heart.

Grades One through Eight got off to a good start as he attended Saint Joseph's parochial school in South Norwalk from 1946 to 1954.

Along with the excellent education that it afforded him, he also got his first and most impressive introduction to discipline. This discipline exercised by the priests and nuns of Saint Josephs had a lasting effect on his remaining life.

Grades Nine through Twelve, 1955 through 1958, Dad was fortunate to be accepted to the electrical course at the J.M. Wright Technical School in Stamford Connecticut. That gave him a sound secondary education as well as the vocation.

Dad loved to tinker. He made me a record player inside of an old bedside table when I was young and gave me my first record, a 45rpm Roberta Flack – "Killing Me Softly" with the flip side, "The First Time Ever I Saw Your Face." Odd choices for a kid.

Dad could've gone in either direction as a young man. Become a criminal or live a life of service to others.

Here in the bedlam of his peers, he made the right choice.

Norwalk had begun a serious drug crisis with heroin and that led Dad to join the Navy, in August 1958.

Tall, lean and with a sweet baby face, he was 17 years young, on August 19, 1958, when he enlisted in the United States Navy in New York City.

The Navy then flew Johnny to Great Lakes, Illinois for 11 weeks of recruit boot camp and trained with company 386 at RTC (Recruit Training Command).

While at RTC he became a member of the drill team and also became a platoon leader. Upon graduation, he was advanced to the rank of seaman apprentice.

Johnny's first post-school duty assignment was as a member of the pre-commissioning crew of the USS Providence.

Dad felt very fortunate that during his duty on the Providence he visited San Juan, Puerto Rico, Haiti, Santa Domingo, Dominican Republic, and Guantánamo, Cuba.

In 1960 into early 1961, the Providence sailed to Veracruz Mexico, Panama City Panama, Costa Rica and Acapulco.

In October 1961 Johnny attended a four-week course then flew to Japan to meet the Providence, which had deployed in September for nine months on a Pacific cruise. There the sailors enjoyed visiting many Japanese cities including Kobe, Kyoto, Hiroshima, and Tokyo. Then it's return tour stopped at Okinawa, Hong Kong, Manila Philippines, and Pearl Harbor Hawaii.

During this time, he had been living with his parents, Harry Sr. & Gladys, at 211 Flax Hill Road in Norwalk CT prior to enlisting in the Navy.

My mother, Kari Walden lived with her family upstairs on the third floor, while my Dad was on the bottom floor. Though they were just friends and not dating, both sets of parents were consistently trying to put them together as a couple.

The first time Johnny saw my Mother, she was clad only in a red swimsuit with plastic inserts in the bathing suit top to make her look vivacious. They had three dates before they decided to get engaged.

Johnny wanted more for himself than the blue-collar life that he grew up in, even though his father was an electronics specialist for American Gramophone and made good money.

His Dad, Harry, was a heavy-handed drinker, as was his Mom Gladys. Particularly when he was drinking, Harry was physically violent to his wife and their three children. Dad's two siblings were brother Harry and sister Mary.

When Harry Jr. went away to war, Johnny was helpful to his wife Roz. Unfortunately, helpfulness turned into comforting and one night after Roz, Dad and his sister Mary went out partying, it was soon obvious that the timing of Harry's departure didn't add up with the pregnancy due date.

It was not long before a young boy by the name of Jerry was born. When Harry Jr. returned to the States, Johnny and Harry went a few rounds but finally sat down and decided that Harry would raise the boy as his own and they would never speak of it again. After my Uncle Harry died his widow Kathi sent me my Dad's badges and we discussed the truth of the story between my Dad and Harry. Up to this point, my sisters and I never knew we had a brother.

Harry and my Dad had an estranged relationship for most of their lives. I have some photos of the two later in life that I have included within the many photographs in this book.

While Dad eventually started the relationship with my Mother, she was stateside while he was away on board his ship. He was sending her all of his extra money and she was spending it, without his knowledge.

Keep in mind that my Mom came from a long line of chaos, as did my Dad. But this book is not about her and their parents.

GONE TOO SOON

Chapter 8

"My parents get married"

On January fourth, 1962, John and Kari got married, and I followed shortly after that in November 1962.

I was born in the Norwalk Hospital in Connecticut, which was the same hospital my father was born in.

My Grandfather Pop brought a clothes pin for my diaper so that he could claim he had a grandson. My brother Joseph would later die as a newborn infant in the same hospital.

It was a time of tragedy for several months, as George Peyton Walden Jr, my maternal Uncle known as Georgie was living in Manhattan at the tender age of sixteen. While working he was beaten up by some hoodlums as the six foot one-inch slight young man could not defend himself, against the five kids.

Georgie went on to join the Navy but was discharged for crashing military equipment. He then moved back home and my mother was asked by the rooming board attendant if Georgie could move in with her and my Dad. My father objected and said "No".

Meanwhile, Georgie was dating an older woman with three kids and she dumped him because of his antics.

Pushing Georgie over the edge, he made his third attempt at suicide by walking straight into a lake and drowned.

Following the death of her brother Georgie, my Mother went into the hospital prematurely with the birth of my brother Joseph. The shock of losing her brother that brought on the birth of Joseph had traumatic consequences and the baby boy only lived another two days.

The following month, my paternal grandfather, Harry Evaneski Sr., who was in constant pain from injuries incurred over his lifetime, died.

Harry who ingested 30-40 aspirins per day, was fixing his car that was up on concrete blocks when the blocks gave way and the car landed on his chest.

Harry hemorrhaged to death as he couldn't clot because of the vast quantities of aspirins that he took.

Following these heartbreaks, in August 1964, Dad was transferred to Treasure Island, California. This island was between San Francisco and Oakland. While continuing his stint in the Navy and after the loss of my brother Joseph, my Mother was soon pregnant again with my middle sister.

At the time, we were living in Oakland California and in January 1965 while still in the Navy John became a member of the Hayward Police Reserve.

June brought the birth of Dad's second daughter and we moved to Hayward California and lived on Willimet Way.

Dad followed his true bliss and sought a career on the police force and on July 17, 1967, he took a position full-time as a Hayward Police Department Officer.

His first assignment was the midnight to 8 AM shift. Learning the ropes he would ride double with the training officer for eight weeks. After riding double on the Police Reserves for two years he felt confident enough to go solo on his first day.

Unheard of at Hayward, this was the first instance of a rookie going solo in the history of the department. Fortunately for all concerned, the situation worked out well and he was off to a good start in his career.

He was constantly known for having a remarkable memory for names, faces, and automobiles of unsavory criminal characters.

Some officers and supervisors were convinced that he had in fact, a photographic memory. Truth be told was that John felt he had a terrible memory. I found this out by recently going through my Dad's estate. There he left behind a large three-ring binder where he recorded every class he ever took.

It also included every job he ever held, so it was like an FYI on John Evaneski. I need to give him credit as the compiler of this Information in this book. He would have enjoyed that.

He programmed his mind so to speak, by going over and over the names, dates of birth, address, vehicle descriptions, and license numbers.

It was important to him to know this information to serve and protect the public and it paid off on numerous occasions with the arrest of wanted fugitives.

Hoping to become a permanent officer in the future he prepared a list by the last name, cataloged in alphabetical order.

It included the full name and description, date of birth, address known associates, brief criminal background in some cases and the photos of known associates. The name list also included license numbers and/or vehicle descriptions of criminals or associates' vehicles as a cross-reference. It was very thorough.

That "Thing", some called a photographic memory was really just a hard working police officer, setting out to do the best job he could possibly do.

He would put 5 to 10 hours a week of his own time developing these lists and updating and otherwise supplementing them that extended over a period from January 1966 to April 1968. Then he reduced the information to a 3 x 5 card system that provided his own personal file and voila! It was that easy.

For all this work, there was positive support from his superiors.

Still, he had to buck the system and really push it to get the vehicle file approved as an official HPD information source and it was well worth it and the number of significant arrests and crime clearances would not have been made without this information.

GONE TOO SOON

Chapter 9

"Leo Durocher"

Leo lived in the same apartment building as I did at the beginning of the 1990s. He had lived there, alone, for quite a while, as I remember. For my first year of knowing him, I had no idea who he was except for "The cranky old dude, that keeps leaving his keys in the mailbox".

The complex was full of mostly older folks, so you ended up helping one person or another on occasions, whether bringing their groceries upstairs, taking out the trash or returning the stranded mail keys to the elderly residents.

Leo was a buddy of Frank Sinatra and once gave me a matchbook from Frank and Barbara's wedding.

He also told me that in his younger days he'd go over to Frank's house and the two of them would shake cans of beer and shoot the two-inch date bugs off of the ceiling.

One day in 1991 the frail Leo, who was once a powerful man in the sports industry left his keys behind again. The building manager Agnes, a frail woman herself, said "Leo's keys are sticking out of the mailbox again. I've tried calling him and he doesn't answer. Will you go and ring his bell?"

I did so and did not receive an answer either, so I checked the garage for his car and found that it was still in his parking spot.

Telling Agnes my findings, she asked me to go around the side and look in his window. Running back to Agnes's apartment, I told her "She needed to call 911 as it looked like the icon was in need of help".

30

Unfortunately, Leo Durocher had passed away at the age of 86 that day. He is now buried at Forest Lawn cemetery in Los Angeles and was posthumously inducted into the baseball Hall of Fame in 1994.

He was like an Uncle to me during those years and we got along surprisingly well. I have seemed to attract old Uncles during my life, though none of them have ever left me anything… except for an old matchbook and some stories about Ol' Blue Eyes.

GONE TOO SOON

Chapter 10

"The Captain of The Love Boat"

In 1991, while working at Saks Fifth Avenue, I was assigned to the accessories and handbag department.

Standing there on that fateful day, I had received a phone call from my doctor's office, who then proceeded to tell me of some test results that came back positive for female cancer.

As I hung up the phone with tears in my eyes, I turned to find Gavin McCloud and his wife Patti standing in front of me.

They immediately grabbed my hands and said, "No matter what it is, let's pray!"

I had never had anyone publicly pray with me, much less a celebrity I did not know. They were beyond kind to me and even had a lovely bouquet of flowers delivered to me at work.

Fortunately for me, I had surgery for the cancer and made a speedy recovery, even without a supportive husband at the time. Larry was about himself, as my Dad would always tell me. And during this period of personal fear, I was left to go through this basically by myself.

After surgery, I continued on at Saks and was blessed to meet many other celebrities. Some, I got to know rather well like Ginger Rogers and Sonny Bono, who ended up being two of my favorites.

Sonny was Mayor of Palm Springs at the time and had opened a restaurant in town when he first moved there. Entertaining and vivacious, Sonny nonetheless, was always welcoming.

I also got to meet Diann Carroll, Robert Wagner, Jill St. John, Frank Sinatra, and Arnold Schwarzenegger.

Additionally, in 1991, I was an extra in the Robert Wagner's Mini-series "False Arrest".

Betty Lou Oppenheim, Jill St. John's Mom, would come and talk to me at work, mostly telling me wild stories, that as a naïve girl stood in amusement that things like that happened.

One day she told me that she had arranged for me a part in a movie being shot in town. I didn't believe her, but then she came walking in and smiling one day and told me to be at this location on a specific day, which in the end, I had to take off from work.

As it turned out, she organized for me to have a role as an "extra", portraying a lady of the night being booked into jail on sex crimes. The movie included Donna Mills. My part was filmed at the Palm Springs Police Station, during a 14-hour long day shoot. I was exhausted when it was done and smiled for days knowing that I was going to be in film forever.

I also knew that my Dad would always be proud of me for this once in a lifetime opportunity, considering that my Dad had been a Vice-Cop.

Chapter 11

An Uncommon Narc! AKA "Undercover Johnny"

In February 1971, Dad was assigned as Acting Detective, followed by the assignment of "Detective in Charge of Vice", July 1971.

Most agencies in Southern Alameda County had small narcotics units and this fact required that all agencies work together.

As Dad always said and as his work records will state "when he was a youngster, he always wanted to be an actor." He said, "I'd always been somewhat of a comedian it's almost mandatory to keep from going crazy in this type of business."

He always told us that he got his chance to be an actor while working on Narcotics investigations.

Doing undercover investigations, was when the actor in Johnny boy came alive.

Or Valdez shines most...

It was said that John gave many convincing performances.

One defendant remarked, "I can't believe it. You're the heat? You deserve an Oscar or at least an Emmy."

He was known to use his imagination to dream up great ways to do stakeouts. This included being inside a cardboard refrigerator box, in the back of the truck doing surveillance during a stakeout.

Dad was always in police mode. When we were young and something would go wrong in the house, Dad would hold court.

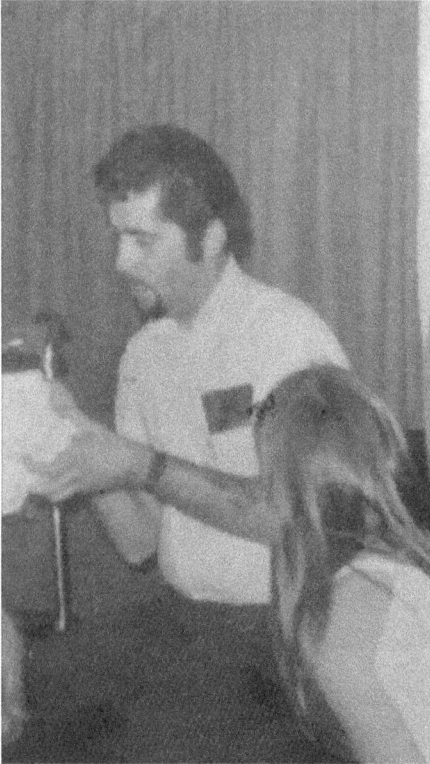

We would have to sit in front of him and listen to the evidence, testify and then he would investigate and give us his ruling.

I remember one time when some change went missing off his dresser. He proceeded over the courtroom. He entered the room doing the comical impression of a Flip Wilson's character. He put on some smooth moves and said, "Here come the judge, Here come the judge!"

If you're younger than 50 you will not understand that impression, so Google it.

More antics. While serving a search warrant in December 1972, John dressed up like Santa Claus that caused him to receive National TV Publicity. It was not the normal way of doing things but it was legal and most of all it worked.

John said he would just do about anything as long as it was legal to get the job done, be successful and lock up the criminals.

Walter Cronkite did a story on the news that night but of course, they couldn't name him on TV since he was undercover.

Cronkite said ...Hayward California. Santa Claus... and the rest was history. Twenty years later after Dad's death, we were able to borrow this video from the Library of Congress. It was short, sweet and about OUR Dad.

In the 1970s a lot of drugs were brought into the area.

During 1973 and 1974 Dad was on detached duty with the United States Department of Justice Drug Enforcement Administration task force in San Francisco.

There, he was allowed to operate in either a local capacity or federal level in the enforcement of the drug laws, as he learned more about joint efforts of various agencies.

Acting as the liaison for the federal agencies and Southern Alameda Counties, he really thrived in the successful investigations that they completed.

During the spring of 1975, Dad was sought out and employed by Chabot College as an instructor for the Administration of Justice Program. He did this part-time and loved teaching narcotic drug enforcement training.

I was in junior high school at this time at Rancho Arroyo in Hayward, right down the street from the college. Someone's older siblings must have been in Dad's class because it was soon circulating throughout the school that my Dad was a cop, "a narcotics cop". Evaneski? It's a common name you know. I couldn't possibly be related. I can't say it hurt my popularity as I was a dork anyway. These are the days before anxiety was diagnosed so I was just simply that weird girl.

GONE TOO SOON

Chapter 12

"Climbing the Ranks"

In July 1975, John was promoted to the rank of Sergeant and assigned to the Patrol Division.

Dad was always highly critical of some of the standard Police practices and said he did not necessarily go along with "that's the way we've always done it" or "that is enough to get by " or similar expression's when it came to professional police work. He would always cringe when reading a sloppy report.

When I read some of his own progress reports, through the Hayward Police Department, his bosses referred to him as "a ball of fire".

There were certain reasonable standards to be met and John said his men will meet those standards, but that he expected improvement which could only be achieved through the setting reasonable goals, coupled with appropriate motivation.

John always tried to share his life experiences in a candid fashion. He would never blow his own horn as he was a dedicated policeman, a leader, not a follower.

A public servant for all of his adult life John served his country and his community in a positive manner always and did so as long as he lived.

In 1969 our youngest sister arrived just as our parents' marriage crumbled even further.

Our parents were both having adulterous affairs at this time and they both started doing something that they claimed they never would do, "drink like their parents".

We are pretty certain that John, fathered other children but for the sake of their privacy, I won't divulge any of that here.

Let's just say that my sisters and I have a game called "could that be our sibling?"

Our parents' marriage already in trouble, ended.

My Mother had an affair with my Dad's co-worker. He is still alive and I'm friendly with his children and it's not my place to break their Father's secret to them.

This was one of the few times I saw my Dad cry. The other time was when our hot water heater blew and destroyed all of my Grandfather's mementos. My Dad who I believed to be a sensitive person, rarely cried.

As the marriage fell apart, I remember our Mother picking us kids up from school and taking us to a pawnbroker so that she could pawn her diamond ring.

I also remember going to the liquor store next to Big Ben's, owned by Big Ben Davison from the Oakland Raiders, a friend of my Dad.

Our mother let us each buy three items of candy for the trip we were taking. One of the things I picked out was a roll of lifesaver butter rums. I saved them the entire weekend we spent at the Holiday Inn, located in San Jose so that I could share them with him upon my return. When I ran into the house, next to his recliner on top of his side lamp table on the left side of his chair was a black felt pen and yellow piece of paper. There was black writing with smudges on the paper as if wet tears had landed on it.

The letter basically said, you have asked me to leave, and I have.

It's hard to be eight years old and to believe you were on a small vacation while your father had to work but to find out you were part of a bigger scheme and you didn't even know it at that time. Believe me, I know he was far from perfect, and a majorly flawed person. But he was still my dad.

Chapter 13

"Weekends with Dad"

Weekends with Dad were a trip.

Sometimes we would be out and Dad would spot a known criminal. He would make a phone call and a police officer would show up and take us children out of the area.

One time, I can recall crawling from one backseat of my Dad's car into the backseat of an undercover police car. Dad was always on duty...always.

Initially, before Dad got remarried, weekends with him would consist of going to the movies and watching completely inappropriate films including Midway, Serpico, and every Godfather movie.

Then we would go to Shakey's Pizza. We always ordered the same kind pepperoni and black olives. Even now, I order pizza that way.

Other times we would go back to Dad's house along with a large bag of tacos from Taco Bell and play poker. As little kids, we did things that were very mature.

Once Dad remarried it all changed. We went looking at model homes and shopping. This is where I learned to negotiate. I can't say I was poor as a kid, but there certainly wasn't any money in the budget for new shoes or new clothes for us children, so I would set out on these weekends to get what I needed.

I wasn't being greedy. It was simply survival. I remembered that once Dad found a pair of shoes that he loved and that loved him, he would buy them in every color he could find. That may have meant he only had that one style of shoe, but he loved them. Growing up like this meant that comfort was a very important thing for him especially his feet.

Dad loved movies and Popcorn - real popcorn. He always cooked it in a pan, on top of the stove. Then he dumped the cooked popcorn into a paper bag to shake the bag to remove the excess oil. Lightly salted and sometimes with butter. Yes, that's my recipe and now it's yours.

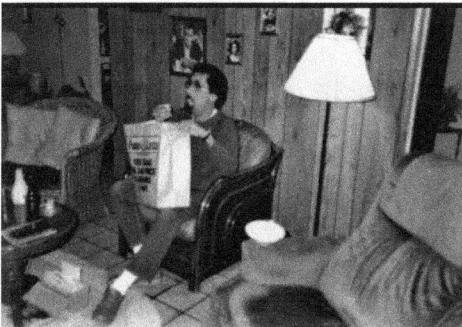

GONE TOO SOON

Chapter 14

"Understanding Life and Dad"

My husband at the time, Larry, opened a tanning salon in the late '80s.

Here I spent most of my life or at least it seemed at that very moment. I would work the front desk, run the tanning schedule, administer European Body Wraps, clean the tanning beds, office spaces and launder the towels. Larry, well he did nothing except act as a big shot and sit on his you know what. Looking back it was pitiful.

The salon was sold in 1989.

About a year prior to selling the store, I was working the front desk and my Stepmother walked in and said, "If you won't come to your father, I will bring him to you!"

Then she handed me a photograph of him.

In my shock, I misunderstood to think that he was there and I went running outside to follow her.

Unfortunately, Larry was running right behind me and started yelling at her to get away from the salon and for me to get back inside.

I looked at him and told him "No, and for him to get back in the store."

Larry was furious as I continued to follow my Stepmother.

Stepping into Rudy's Pizza, she was there to attend a nearby wedding, without my father, which I didn't learn about till I sat with her and her friends.

Larry, the ever possessive man, kept looking in the window and motioning me to leave, which I ignored but later, paid for it with verbal abuse.

The irony is that Larry never met my Dad or Stepmother but would tell me that my Dad did not Love me and that he was disappointed in me, which after a while I believed to my dismay.

Sometimes I would walk down the street from the Salon so as not been seen by Larry in order to call my Dad and ask him to please call me. I wanted Larry to see that my Dad really Loved me.

He refused, which was again another disappointment in my life.

In hindsight now, I believe he knew I was in a terrible domestic relationship and didn't want to get involved.

Dad was not a game player. He expected you to be straight forward about what you wanted out of him.

As an adult, that is now obvious to me but as a young naïve woman, I found it very hard to negotiate a relationship with him let alone Larry.

He was a very busy man living his own life. Even when we were kids, he was not really into parenting us once our parents were divorced. It was as if he divorced us as well.

GONE TOO SOON

Chapter 15

"February 18th, 1992"

Dad had gone to the doctor and received a clean bill of health for his recent hernia surgery.

Upon returning home Dad asked his wife for his favorite dinner prior to heading into Oakland that Tuesday night. Hamburger steak and sliced cucumbers. She laughed and told him to make it himself. Years later, she told me how much she regretted that.

He went to work and chatted with the owner of the club about picking up some extra shifts. He then ate some Jerk Chicken and started playing some music.

At 9:25 PM, while on stage, two young black men in ski masks burst into the nightspot spraying the small space with assault weapons.

Shooting Dad first because they did frequent the Bos'n and knew that Dad was probably carrying a firearm.

Dad fell against his DJ equipment and speakers.

When the Oakland police and the Alameda County Sheriff's department showed up on the scene, it was one of the most horrific massacre's in the history of Northern California.

In the days that followed, the story that emerged in the press was that "it was a hit on Dad". And there were plenty of stories that were wild.

For some relief, the subjects were caught later that week at the race track as we all converged on Fremont and Hayward to say goodbye to our father.

I remember walking through the door of the Chapel of the Chimes. It was an open casket which surprised me. He did not look like himself. My Mother could be heard in the parking lot laughing. Apparently, she was so nervous about being there that she was introducing herself as Rod's first wife. Folks were looking at her like she was some bizarre crazy lady. Like, "Who the hell is Rod?" He was her current husband.

So it's this awkward situation, that is sad and horrible and then you've got this ex-wife greeting grieving people.

Reminiscing my last time I saw Dad alive was at the Los Angeles International Airport as he was flying to Jamaica.

I met his flight from the Bay area to LA and we were going to have a meal together. He got off the airplane and was extremely tan with an overdone glow, and blue jeans with a white shirt, sporting loafers and no socks.

We were supposed to have a meal together but ended up in the bar. Even today, I would say that he was pretty obnoxious as he had already been drinking. He was very thin and basically his conversation was about getting on board the plane and fly to Jamaica.

I took the airport shuttle over to air Jamaica to say goodbye to him. I never thought that this would be the last time I'd see him alive. And that the next time it would be in his coffin. Murdered at 51.

The court case against those who committed this crime was very long and the first case ended in a hung jury. But the prosecutor, Mr. Anderson, fought a good fight.

I now feel bad, as I had called Mr. Anderson every day during both trails and every year after that on the day of Dads murder.

I wanted to thank him for all his hard work and to let him know that not a day goes by that I don't thank him for his tenacity. He told me he would retire next year before February 18 but assured me that my Dad was smiling down on us. We then said our goodbyes.

In the end, I don't want to discuss these people, we all have our own God to stand in front of someday.

In 1994 a song came out based on a poem I wrote the day my Father died. It was on a reggae CD that barely saw the light of day and that is okay with me as I have regrets in allowing something so personal, to be coerced out of me by relatives of my first husband.

GONE TOO SOON

Chapter 16

"MacGyver"

Richard Dean Anderson

1995 Palm Springs, California

At that time, I was working in Palm Springs at the Ann Taylor store, as the assistant store manager.

Every time I would go to lunch, I'd tell the staff that I would be back in an hour unless I ran into Richard Dean Anderson and then I will be at the Hyatt!

On this particular day, I went to meet the man I was seeing after filing for divorce from Larry. He was a Vice-President for the only record company in the city. We were in love and had plans to marry.

Sitting within a street view, we were having lunch at a restaurant that opened up on to Palm Canyon Drive, which is the main thoroughfare of the city.

After returning from the restroom, I witness my dream come true, Richard Dean Anderson, walking by with another man and a woman. Michael saw my face and said, "Go ahead, I know you have to!"

So I am following Mr. Anderson down Palm Canyon Drive before you can snap your fingers. I am pretty sure I see Richard walk into a tee shirt shop on the left-hand side of the street and I walk in and meander my way through the store to no avail. However, as I head for the front door to leave, he is standing there.

Panicked, I immediately turn and look into the store window from the outside as if I'm searching for something. With my back to Richard, he walked over to me and taps my shoulder. You guessed it, "I'm thinking he can feel the heat, and my thoughts go to my staff to tell them, "I'll be at the Hyatt!"

Shyly I turn around and say "Hello".

He smiles at me with a kind of "fatherly grin" and says, "Your skirt is tucked inside your pantyhose".

Eek! I said, "Thank you", but inside my brain, I am cursing myself for being in this situation. How could I be that silly at this specific time in my life? I was so embarrassed. The one time…

But lessoned learned ladies, always check your skirt!

Anyway, I am sure he told his friends and they had a good laugh, but that was the day in1995 that I fell out of Love with Richard Dean Anderson and back "In Love" with my own Life.

GONE TOO SOON

Chapter 17

"The Tree"

A tree was planted in front of the Hayward Police Department for my Dad. He was cremated and a plaque for his memorial was placed out front.

A photograph of the tree is included in the photo section of this book. There have been many caretakers over the years and they know that I appreciate them.

Interesting, at one point the original tree died and so another one was planted in its place. To me, that meant it was another reminder that I needed to move on, as I am so much more than a murder victim's daughter.

In 1995 I finally got divorced but by 1996, I was remarried and expecting a baby. I married the

President of the record label that released the CD that my "song" was on.

In 1996 also brought my entry into the music industry as a sales & marketing representative. This lent itself to new challenges and I found myself taping into the A & R (Artists and Repertoire) side of the business.

One such label we signed to our record distribution company was Rodney King and his label Straight Out.

This was just as Rodney had won the lawsuit against the LA Police and we attended the urban radio convention in Palm Springs.

We found both empathy and sympathy for Rodney since he was surrounded by people who only wanted to take from him.

We asked him when we could, without the leeches "What the beating did to him, besides the scars?"

We found him to be very childlike and sweet. He would not ever let me walk to my car alone and was always a gentleman.

Once I had to take him to Simi Valley where the trial took place and he was very nervous.

We laughed on the way back in traffic because the folks in the restaurant thought he was the rapper, Coolio.

I'm certain you never heard anyone refer to Rodney as a gentleman, but you had to know him after the beating. Sadly his life ended with more chaos, but I will always have a soft spot in my heart for him.

GONE TOO SOON

Chapter 18

"More Music Please Became My Calling"

My life at that time consisted of traveling to Tower Records and Virgin Megastores calling on the buyers. I remember my first store, the iconic Tower Records Sunset location and the buyer, Larry King.

Larry was the coolest. He took this still newbie music business person and trusted me. This really secured my relationship with the rest of the store buyers as I was soon known for being straight up with no hype. I never oversold a release and if I said buy more, it meant I knew what I was talking about.

This is where the fun began!

Doing in-store appearances with artists was always a blast, watching the artists and the consumer fans interact.

Concerts, tours and moments I cannot believe I was able to experience, even today. After the death of Tupac and Biggie, the Urban music scene was bigger than ever and I was writing huge orders for Ludacris, Lil Jon, and the Ying Yang twins.

I was invited by my friends from Pat Speer and Brian Shafton of Pacific Coast One Stop to the studio of Snoop (Calvin) Dogg late one night and spent time talking to an older man that was hanging out. It turns out that he was Snoop's Uncle.

He told me he was the brother of Snoop's Mother and appeared in a video that showed Snoop as an older man which was really the Uncle.

According to the Uncle, Snoop's name was coined by his Mom, because he watched Peanut Cartoons.

I have no idea if he was pulling my leg, but the Uncle was charming and entertaining.

It was a blast to attend this recording though I am sure that we all had contact highs, even if we did not indulge.

Snoop was on Priority Records at the time and I was given a framed picture of myself, Pat Speer and the famed rapper. I also received a Priority Records baseball jacket.

I ended up giving the jacket to a lifeguard at a military base pool that my husband and I went to. He apparently lost his shirt during the day, so I felt sorry for him and gave it to him. One must always share things in life if you can.

Another time, Tony Iommi had released his self-titled album in October 2000.

The release party was held at Sharon and Ozzy Osborne's offices in Los Angeles, which was a fun event to attend with Pat Speer and Brian Shafton.

Many people from the industry were there that night including Henry Rollins, Dave Grohe, Billy Corgan, among others.

Sitting on the very large couch and overstuffed chairs, these guys were signing each other's promos, laughing it up. Mine still hangs in our office.

My friend Carl, from Norwalk Distribution, accidentally caught his hair on fire from the many candles that lit up the dim room, during the casual and intimate gathering.

Another moment in time occurred when I had the opportunity to hang out with Brian Wilson at the Music Biz convention where Brian received "The Chairman's Award."

GONE TOO SOON

Chapter 19

"The Italian Godfather"

Doesn't everyone want an Italian Godfather?

I remember growing up thinking my Godfather lived in a castle in Italy...

In 1960, Dad meets Guerino Felicioni, from the Italian Navy. The two of them were based at the Navy Base at Great Lakes, taking classes. The Base was just north of Chicago, where they became very close friends and would take the train to the city to explore on an occasional Saturday.

When I was born, Dad and Mom made Guerino my Godfather. Sometimes, he would come to the States all dressed in his uniform to see my parents and me. Once my Mother saw him tucking money inside my clothes, which is an Italian tradition. However, my Mother flipped out on him and accused him of something terrible. Because of this he never came back because he was very hurt, and I was so sad and never forgave my Mom for this.

When my Dad was alive, he wanted me to find Guerino and I wrote letters to the Italian Navy, including the consulate in the States along with the Italian Navy with no replies.

When the computer age came around, my second and current husband looked up the information and brought me a phone number. As simple as that. I called the number and asked for Guerino!

"Felicioni?" the man said Felicioni, "Yes Guerino no!"

I tried to explain who I was and that I was looking for my Godfather. The man said you call back one hour. I thought for a while that maybe it was the last name, that I had rung up the wrong person. So I decided to wait the hour and when I called back the man with the deep Italian accent said "LAURA!!!"

We barely understood each other but it was him, my Godfather, after all these years. He was heartbroken to find that his friend, my Dad, had died. But we spoke about the good times without reminiscing about anything bad.

Since then, we have been in each other's life, writing, emailing and through Facebook our daily lives. I have felt blessed to connect with someone who knew my Dad and who has shared with me those early days. And though his wife of fifty plus years has recently passed, we have continued to stay connected and will do so as long as we can.

GONE TOO SOON

Chapter 20

"Folkways"

In 2007, I was hired to work for the iconic Folk label in Washington DC, which lasted until 2017.

When the industry of CDs slowed and the label had not jumped into the Vinyl game, my position came to an end. Saddened, but I eventually came to accept my new role as Guardian of my own destiny and Grandmother, I've progressed just nicely, Thank you.

Over these past ten years, I was blessed to travel across the country, meeting the likes of Melissa Etheridge, Cyndi Lauper, Taylor Swift, and so many others. It was the time of my life.

You never get over the ending of lives, you only get on with it.

You might ask yourself why am I telling all of these personal stories of involvement with celebrities and musicians?

It is basically to share that even though terrible things happen, really good things can emerge.

I got re-married, had a child and went on to have a career that I loved.

I was honored to speak publicly and to lecture at a University Music Program about my own experience and how the business operates.

And now with this book, I am sharing my Dad with everyone.

He was a character, a man of the people, a public servant and a "ham at heart", and the one thing that binds us together besides blood is that we never give up!

GONE TOO SOON

Chapter 21

"Another Death"

In February 2018, I received a phone call from the Clark County corners office in Las Vegas Nevada.

The woman on the other end asked me if I was related to a man that they had in their Facility.

It turned out to be my ex-husband and as I held the phone in my hand, I repeated what the woman said to me, "Larry's Dead!".

A bit in shock, I found out that he had died from complications of the flu and they could not find anyone to claim him.

I told her what family information I still remembered.

The woman asked me if I could claim him and I said: "No, since I no longer had any connections to him."

But I told her that he still had a brother that was alive, although he may not claim him either as he was a very bad man.

I did end up calling back a few weeks later, just to make sure everything was taken care of.

Later, I did have several conversations with old friends of his and found out that he had scammed more than one out of large amounts of money.

This spanned my memory that about 10 years ago, I had received a call from what I believe to be the Feds searching for him or seeking information about him.

Looking back now, I must have become a nicer person because one part of me was very sad that no one wanted to claim him since there was no obituary as if he had never existed.

Somehow Larry's death became important and connected with the here and now as I wrote about my Dad.

GONE TOO SOON

Chapter 22

"The Final Chapter"

Fast forward to now a quarter of a century and the phone call.

On the other end, a gentleman introduced himself as Frank Serpico. Thee Frank Serpico! "What?"

He told me the story about a documentary that was made about him, a couple of years ago.

Upon looking for some photographs that the studio was in need of, Frank came across a box. A year or so later while re-filing everything in the box, a letter fell out. It was unopened and addressed to Frank Serpico attention in care of Artists Entertainment Complex film company, that had made the movie Serpico. Then it was sent over and directed to Frank's publisher.

Eventually, the box of things was given to Frank and since it was a very busy time in his life, he put the box aside.

When I had a conversation with him on that day in September 2018, he apologized for never reading the letter or getting back to me.

In the letter, I told him how much he meant to my father. How my father had tried to emulate his life. How he was obviously obsessed with the movie, "Serpico", and that "Valdez" was Dad's alter ego.

Frank told me that the reason why he called was that he felt almost as if he was channeling my Dad.

I told him about the book and how I've been torn about writing it and he said obviously Dad knew that and that this call was to encourage me.

Dad knew for me, there had to be a BIG push. Interesting as a young girl, I had never written to Al Pacino only to Frank Serpico...

That is how life becomes full circle. I know with every ounce of my being that my Dad is smiling down upon each of us that read this book.

He probably thinks it's crazy and wild that someone would write a book about him much less his daughter.

Characters this large cannot come from someone's imagination. They are so far and few between and must come from real life.

Dedicated to John Evaneski and Frank Serpico

The end.

www.ingramcontent.com/pod-product-compliance
Lightning Source LLC
Chambersburg PA
CBHW032033090426
42741CB00006B/800